RELATIONSHIPS

101

Forbidden Secrets Of Love, Sex, Happiness, & The Male-Female Dynamic, Explained

Rone John M. Bulaong

DISCLAIMER

Readers are to make their own independent inquiries from appropriate professionals before acting on any information. Testimonials do not constitute a guarantee, warranty, or prediction as to the effects of any services, lifestyle changes, etc., contained within this book. Readers of any contained information assume all civil or other risk for their actions related to this book and by utilizing this book and contained information release the author of all claims, damages, and liabilities. All information included within this book is protected under copyright law and all other relevant forms of intellectual property rights are reserved.

Copyright © 2015 Rone John Bulaong
ISBN: 1514131609
ISBN-13: 978-1514131602

"To Those Whom Are Free And Independent Beings Whom Consider Themselves The Ultimate Arbiter Of Their Own Existence, This Book Is For You."

ACKNOWLEDGEMENTS

A lot of the work here I've assimilated from my friend and mentor, Johnny Soporno. You should check him out at JohnnySoporno.com. He's probably the only person in the world that if he were to correct me or say I'm wrong on a matter, I'd actually consider correcting myself. I couldn't say the same about anyone else (just think of any world-renowned guru), in my long tenure as a dating and relationships coach and neurolinguist. To say that what we teach and propagate are different would be a dishonor.

TABLE OF CONTENTS

INTRODUCTION

I'm going to go over some fundamental aspects of your thinking that may actually be ruining your relationships, inhibiting your chances of having a happy life for which you are pleased and satisfied with yourself, and is causing you to feel shame, guilt, and unhappiness over things that you have no reason to be feeling those things.

In fact, these ideas I'm going to talk about are so simple and banal, most everyone miss it… but, they go back to the very roots of your thinking. They were programmed in your mind from a time in your childhood when you didn't even think to ask any questions and you just took what the "authority figure" (grownups) said as absolute truth.

When you really understand what you're about to read, you'll begin to discover how you can truly have more incredible relationships with more people. You'll feel better about yourself and the things you act on that you used to feel shame, guilt, and fear of doing… and you'll discover how you can just be happy all the time and better yet, you'll know how to help other people feel happy without compromising your own integrity.

If you're a man reading this, propagate these ideas to women and they will love you for doing so. If you're a woman reading this, you will begin to truly understand yourself deeper… you will discover how you actually live in a world where you are enslaved by society (you are in a "double-bind" which I'll go into later…). You'll find out how you can begin to free yourself from this oppression and begin to live by your own rules, feel good about yourself, feel good about your innate desires, and have an amazing, fun, and happy life where you get to live it as big as you want!

These fundamental truths won't even surprise you. You'll simply immediately recognize, "Hey, that's reasonable and true!" Most people that hear what I'm about to tell you recognize it immediately and they usually say something like, "You're right! I've wasted all my life believing in something I didn't actually really 'know' to be true. Instead, most of what I know are just things I heard and not think to debate any deeper."

For some people, this information fights with their ego for a few days or weeks (because that's the job of the ego… to not be diminished – but remember, you aren't your ego), and then they come to comfort with it later and realize it's true, as you'll discover… the facts that were given were truly logical, based on irrefutable reason, and have always been self-evident.

UNFOUNDED MISCONCEPTIONS

We live in a society where most of what we know are based on unfounded misconceptions – things we thought were absolute truth, but upon retrospection are illogical, insane, and obsolete – makes no sense and has no reason to exist… and I'll prove it to you.

Women in our society who do what they want for their own reasons are taught to feel shame, guilt, and develop hatred for themselves. This is absolutely insane and hateful towards women. Not only that, it also sucks for men.

To put it into the correct context, I'd like you to first think about something for a moment…

When you put gas in your car, do you leave your car on or do you turn it off? Most people say they turn their car off, and I ask, "Why?"

Their reason is because either, "The car might explode", "Something might go wrong", "I don't know. Everyone's doing it and it's what I've been taught." "The sign says so," but nobody seems to know the real reason why they do it.

Here's the interesting bit. The only sparks that occur in a car happen underneath the spark plug cover on the engine, where it's safe for combustion to occur – this is in fact what drives the car. If sparks were to happen anywhere else in the vehicle, cars would be exploding at random at any time!

Funny thing… in 1973/'74 we had both regular gas and unleaded gas. Regular gas had lead in it to help the engine run better. At that time, the US started producing cars with catalytic converters for which leaded gas would wreak havoc… so most cars started using unleaded gas. Meanwhile, during that same time, there was an oil crisis where the US sided with a country that was at war with another country that exported oil to the US.

So those countries had an oil embargo and stopped exporting oil to the US.

Gas prices rose. Gas station owners began to consider how they'd be able to afford this...

At that time, there were gas station attendants whose sole job it was to stand by the pump and put gas in people's cars. The law had to be passed to turn off the vehicle before putting gas because otherwise, that poor gas station attendant would not only inhale carbon monoxide but also lead.

When the gas station owners figured out that gas would be more affordable if they got rid of the gas station attendant – and 'Self-Serve' came about, there was no longer any reason for that law to exist! Yet, people still seem to keep believing it without recognizing the reasons behind why we do the things that we do.

We grow up believing things because we learned them at a young age when we didn't think to ask any questions. We saw the grown-ups as "authority" and we never considered the possibility that things would be any other way as they're presented to us. We end up believing things that are not true, we end up believing things that are obsolete, don't make any sense, illogical, and believe things that have no reason for its existence.

Have you ever been told, "Don't sit 6 feet or closer to the TV"? That came about because way back then, televisions were only 12 inches wide. The only way that the grownups could watch television without their kids blocking the view was to tell them don't sit close to the TV or it'll ruin your eyes! (We sit closer to our laptops and they've got more power than old-style TVs).

Now with these basic foundational realizations in mind – that we believe things that have no reason to exist, that aren't true – let me talk about "cultural misogyny"...

WOMEN HAVE BEEN DEALT A HARD HAND

Women in our society are taught to believe things that are illogical. In our society and internationally, there is a "sexual cartel".

A cartel is made up of an oligopoly, like OAPEC (The Organization of Arab Petroleum Exporting Countries) where they produce the same product for which they agree upon a certain price so as not to undercut anyone else. Inevitably someone in the cartel always undercuts someone else because it benefits them (that's why Iraq would roll in with tanks to Kuwait in 1990).

Our society has a sexual cartel – a hidden set of communicated instructions that teach women to believe they have to behave a certain way and not 'behaving' in this way is undercutting the sexual cartel.

Women in our society are in a Double Bind. This is a paradox that means, "I'm damned if I do, and damned if I don't."

Women in our society who have sex are divided into 2 categories. On one side is a woman who does things for her own reasons. She has sex with a man without asking for anything in exchange - not for long-term security, for a relationship, or for any kind of value. She has sex with him for her own reasons.

Maybe she's a news reporter and she's traveling the world and can't "settle down" right now. Maybe she's a powerful CEO of a company and doesn't want to settle down. Maybe she's a marine biologist who does research around the world and doesn't want to be held down by a relationship.

Her peers, her aunts, her parents will shout at her and say, "When are you gonna settle down? You're going to grow old, and unattractive, and infertile." They say all these things because they don't know what they're saying. They condemn her. They look down on her.

Think about that... a woman who has sex with a man for her own reasons without asking for anything in exchange... maybe it's because she just likes him, she thinks he's cute, she's horny, she's bored, she wants to have fun, he reminds her of someone, whatever it is, it's for her own reasons. Society will judge her, condemn her and say, "You have no self-respect! You give it away for nothing!"

And they will call her a nasty, evil, four-letter word. Have you figured out what that word is?

The women I ask that question to, always come up with the word 'slut'.

Slut doesn't actually have any meaning. When a guy calls a girl a slut, it just means she's sleeping with more men than he'd like her to. When a woman calls another woman a slut, it is the most hurtful, cutting thing she can call another woman.

It means she is giving away for free what her sisters have to charge for. SHE IS UNDERCUTTING THE CARTEL!

When a woman wears a more revealing article of clothing – maybe it's a lower cut top or a higher cut skirt, other women will look at her, condemn her, and call her a slut because she's catching the attention of those men that they have to 'sell' themselves to, to pretend they aren't that 'easy', that they wouldn't give it up too easily because she's been taught all her life that her value is in her vagina. She's been taught to never give it up on the first date and make a man work for it so that he recognizes and prices her value.

So inevitably, these women who does as she pleases, whom are emancipated, and do things for their own reasons, recognize that their peers will judge and condemn them, so they stop hanging out with women, maybe has very few special female friends, and has more men friends.

Now if you think about it also, if you were to say to a man who does things for his own reasons and has sex with a woman for nothing in return, and you told him, "You give it all away for nothing! You have no self-respect!" … to a man, that would sound absolutely ridiculous and wouldn't make sense at all.

A man who has a long list of partners is called a stud, and a woman who has a long list of partners is called a slut?

Do you see where this entire paradigmatic stupidity breaks down?

THE OTHER KIND
OF WOMAN

Okay, going back, if on one side there's the woman who does what she wants for her own reasons, for nothing in exchange, then on the other side is the woman who has sex only for something in exchange… and there's a word we call a woman who only has sex for something in exchange - who only has sex for value, (she charges for it)…

What do you call this woman?

For all intents and purposes… we'll call this woman, who only has sex for value, a whore.

Here's the interesting part… in our society there are two kinds of 'whores': there's a low-status whore and a high-status whore. The low-status kind might say, "Well… he paid for my trip to Hawaii, he helped me with my taxes, he paid for my kids school, he bought me a car, he pays for my rent… so I'll have sex with him." Or, maybe it's, "Well, he gave me $300, so I'll have sex with him."

That's the low-status kind. Then, there's the high-status kind, which we will call a "contract whore."

This kind of woman asks for an exorbitant price for her exclusive sexual access. She asks for a contract stating she will provide him sexual access, and no one else (not publicly anyway), as long as he contracts to provide her and her offspring with security for the rest of their life and he cannot have sex with anyone else.

There's a nasty, evil, 4-letter word we call this woman too.

We call her a wife.

So this is how messed up society has stylized itself over thousands of years. The woman who does things for her own reasons, who is the ultimate arbiter of how to live her life, who does things because it suits her, has sex for nothing in return, is looked down on and branded as a traitor to her gender… and the woman who only has sex for a contract of security is deemed as appropriate behavior.

EMANCIPATION

If you're a woman reading this, emancipate yourself from the sexual cartel. Begin to recognize that security, the one that women were taught all their life to depend on firstly from their father, then their husband, for… the kind of security that you crave isn't something you need from anyone else. A girl essentially becomes a woman when she recognizes that she provides for her own security and forgoes her need to please people.

This is why women in our society have an overwhelming need to please other people and not do or say things that won't please other people. This is because culturally, for the last several thousands of years, women were essentially treated as property of men. They were always taught to "please their sponsor," whom firstly was her father, then it was her husband.

Realize that for the majority of history, women did not always have freedom of choice as to whom they'd marry, rather, it was a vending off from father to husband.

While men were raised with men's honor codes – that their word is their bond – women aren't raised the same way.

She's taught all her life to please her sponsor, whether it's daddy or hubby. She quickly learns this very important foundational philosophy, "What daddy doesn't know won't hurt him." She quickly learns "equivocation."

Essentially, she quickly begins to realize, not being caught misbehaving is the same thing as behaving. Not being caught telling a lie is the same thing as telling the truth.

Equivocation is changing the meaning of things. It's the same thing as when Bill Clinton said, "I did not have sexual relations with that woman." You see, to him, getting a blowjob was not considered as having sexual relations.

It's for this reason that when asked, both men and women agree, women are crazy… or, "You can't trust women." That's not true… you CAN trust woman. You can trust women to be women! Realize that when you're taught that truth is equal to false, white equals black, one equals zero… you can pretty much make sense of anything. When things that are illogical are taught to be true, you can make anything true. When you're taught to behave in such a way that goes against everything you naturally are, you cannot possibly function, sanely and logically, in that society.

And this is how messed up society has raised women, and if you're a woman, you must emancipate yourself.

HOW THIS CULTURAL MISOGYNY CAME ABOUT

10,000-11,000 years ago, at our last significant ice age, humans discovered something that changed everything… we discovered agriculture. Before that time, humans were hunters and gatherers.

We lived in small groups and moved around to places where there were food and shelter. While hunting and gathering was very inefficient – you could kill a large mammoth but without refrigeration, most of it goes to waste – agriculture was very efficient – we could stay in one place, grow crops and farm animals, using only a small amount of manpower.

With agriculture came the concept of ownership. Before agriculture, we simply had our survival tools, moved around a lot, and essentially shared everything with our tribe. Upon discovering agriculture, the idea of ownership and property became important because we would reap what we sowed and harvested.

This new idea that in the same way that you put seed into fertile soil and reap harvest, if you put seed into woman, you reap harvest… for which could help till the land for the coming seasons and inherit property. It was because of this that it was very important for men to know that their children were their own and for thousands of years, especially the last 3-4,000 years, men have come up with ways to own their women and to make sure their children were their own.

It takes around 30 days for one rotation of moon. A "honeymoon" was created so that the woman was sequestered away from other men after marriage, for the man to know that his new bride whom he'd have sex for the first time, would for sure bear *his* child.

This is why virginity was so priced for so long. If a woman were not demonstrably a virgin after marriage, she would be stoned to death in front of the family house. They've had things such as chastity belts, for which the woman's vagina was held under lock and key, literally, by the owner. Nowadays, most men wouldn't think to marry a woman unless he's had sex with her first.

All of it was so the husband could know his child was his own. This is also the reason why only the first born child could be heir to throne – the first born child, conceived during the "honeymoon", could be the child that were for sure the husbands.

For thousands of years we've had harems and harem guards. Harem guards were castrated and guarded the harem owner's wives. This was inefficient because nobody would really volunteer to cut off their balls to become harem guards. So some very "clever" men came together and came up with new rules.

What is the one thing that everyone would fear and whose rules would follow?

God.

This was the concept that if you "sin", you might not get punished while you're alive but when you die, you're really going to get it in terrifying ways.

Throughout human history, we've always had gods. Humans have always wanted to know the meaning of things. When they looked up at the sky and the sun came up, there must be something that makes it happen; there must be a sun god. When it's raining, the gods must be sad. When there's a storm, the gods must be angry. The sun revolves around the earth; the earth must be the center of the universe. The earth is flat.

You see, science and technology has only been around for a couple of thousand years. It's relatively *very* new compared to human's evolution. In fact, it wasn't that long ago when anyone that came up with the notion that the Earth wasn't the center of the universe for which might undermine the belief of religion, would be sentenced to jail. Remember, for a very long time, church was not separate from the state.

These "clever" men came up with certain rules to create persistence out of the idea of owning women. There are '10 commandments'.

The first 5 "rules" (commandments) were created so that these rules would persist and continue on. Things such as, thou shalt not worship any other god, keep the Sabbath day holy, etc.

These were important in the same way that in cult psychology, everyone must adhere to rules to ensure their beliefs persist in their mind. These are things like going to meetings every week or having set times for worshipping their gods.

Remember that anything you know is true doesn't require your believing it. You just know it to be true. The next 3 rules are just good rules for ANY society; thou shalt not steal, thou shalt not kill. But pay attention to the next two rules because they are very telling…

One rule was for the man.
One rule was for the woman.

For the woman it was, "Thou shalt not commit adultery", so she doesn't have sex with other men whom she wasn't married. For the man it was, "Thou shalt not covet thy neighbor's wife", so he wouldn't steal other men's property.

CONDITIONAL AND UNCONDITIONAL LOVE

Love is the central theme to my existence.

A lot of how we currently view love is based on how culture has stylized itself over thousands of years. It's very important to really recognize what love is. I like to say I don't believe in conditional love.

Conditional love is saying, "Because I love you, therefore you cannot love anyone else romantically. If you do things that were not part of our 'agreement', I'll no longer love you." Do you see how this came from the idea of ownership?

"Belonging" is a misnomer.

For example, I bought my wristwatch, it's worth several thousand dollars, it's "mine". My wristwatch CANNOT belong to me because it cannot feel the emotion of 'longing'. If my watch were to end up in someone else's wrist, it wouldn't care. I would. So, rather, I long for my watch. I 'belong' to my watch.

I have an amazing, incredible, beautiful girlfriend whom I love and cherish and adore. I can never say she belongs to me because I have no say in her emotion of longing. Rather, I can say that I belong to her because I long for her. Only she can say she belongs to me when she feels a longing for me.

In first Greek philosophies, love was divided into different kinds. There was Eros; sexual romantic love… Storge; familial love… Philia; love for your friends… and Agape; unconditional love for mankind.

Unconditional love (as opposed to conditional love) is my wanting for my beloved's happiness intrinsic to my own.

How much do you want for your happiness? I'd bet it's one of the most important things to you. Now, wanting that same kind of utmost happiness and joy for your beloved… that's unconditional love.

In fact, any lack of wanting for your beloved's happiness is a demonstration of your lack of love for her.

Jealousy is a compound emotion of fear and rage.

It's very important to remember that we're born with only two emotions: love and fear (and only 2 fears: fear of falling and fear of loud noises). Any other emotion you feel comes from either love or fear.

Jealousy is your ego shouting at you and saying, "If I gave my beloved choice, she might not choose me!" So you feel rage that you feel this fear of loss.

In fact, I let my beloved do whatever makes her self-happy, self-validated, self-successful, and self-actualized, without any notion of jealousy and no ideas of ownership.

I say "self-happy" because while most people tend to believe happiness is something to be 'gotten' ("I'll be happy when…"), the truth is happiness is something we create for ourselves.

The reason most people believe happiness is something that 'comes' from outside of them is because when we were babies, we were only either comfortable or uncomfortable. When we were comfortable we were happy. When we weren't, we saw the pattern that whenever we cried out of unhappiness, we 'received' something that was given to us and it made us happy. We thought that we could only become happy when we 'get' something.

The truth is, just the same as there are people that can feel miserable for no reason at all, you can feel happy for absolutely no reason at all because it's something you yourself create.

If you took someone who's a happy, positive, content person and he became a paraplegic… five years later you'll see a happy, positive, content paraplegic sitting on a wheelchair.

If you took someone who's a cynic, negative, unhappy person and you gave him a million dollars… five years later you'll see a cynic, negative, unhappy person with money in his bank and angry because everyone just likes him for his money – and he'll probably be right.

So what does it mean, really?

How could you not get jealous?

Do you not have boundaries in your relationship?

Could you possibly romantically love more than one person?

You wouldn't get jealous if she slept with someone else?

In order for that idea, of letting my beloved do what makes her happy, even if what's making her happy is not with me, we must understand not only our true nature, wants, and desires… but also what makes us intrinsically "happy".

THE TWO RULES

In my relationships I have two incredible rules that perpetuate happiness and unconditional love. These are my only two rules. Any other rules like 'always wear condoms'; those aren't rules, they're just common sense.

Rule #1: I Will Never Be Any Woman's Only Male Lover

Now this doesn't mean that she has to be committing the act, but she actually has to at least try to audition other men. I like to put it in this metaphor:

I am, metaphorically, a steakhouse and all I provide is steak. I do provide amazing, great steak, but that's all I provide. If I told my beloved, I will give you your favorite steak, filet mignon, anytime you want! Breakfast, lunch, dinner, midnight snack, morning snack, afternoon snack... anytime! As long as you never, ever, ever, ever have anything else...

While in the beginning that sounds like fun... soon, something begins to occur in the relationship: the notion of being and feeling taken for granted.

A few weeks go by and she no longer looks forward to eating her favorite filet mignon because she knows she's gonna get it. She no longer appreciates it for what it is. She now only eats it for 'fuel'. Anything you have, as much as you want of, loses its value.

At the same time, I no longer have any incentive to make the best steak I could make because I know she's gonna take it whether or not how good I make it. We now eventually both feel taken for granted.

Interestingly, being and feeling taken for granted is the death knell of any loving, worthwhile relationship.

Time goes by and she begins to crave pasta, quesadilla, Filipino, Chinese, sushi!... anything else but steak.

Rule #1 makes it so we don't ever take each other for granted. Even if she says, "I don't care if you see other women, I'll only sleep with you", I wouldn't allow it because she'll begin taking me for granted.

Women are taught from an early age that when they grow up, they're going to find a tiger. He's going to be masculine, strong, handsome, a leader, powerful, kind, sweet, great in bed, sexually romantic, and interested in her and her alone. She finds this tiger and shouts, "I found my tiger!!"

She takes this tiger home, sleeps with the tiger, and wakes up the next morning only to find the tiger has gone! She cries, "Where's my tiger!?"

A tiger will do tiger things.

Eventually she finds another tiger and this time she takes him home and locks the doors and the windows for the tiger not to escape. Soon enough, the tiger stops being a tiger and becomes a big, despondent, housecat.

She cries, "Oh no, what happened to my tiger!?" Most everyone doesn't know this about the male and female dynamic... the more a female has satisfying sex, the more she craves it.

On the other hand, the more a man has sex with the same woman, the less he has a craving for it.

When you put a bull in a paddock full of heifers, he will have sex with each one in turn. He won't say, "Well Bessie was good, I'll go do Bessie again." A bull does his job.

What arouses a man is novelty.

On the other hand, the woman doesn't understand the nature of her hormones, mostly in part because she wasn't raised to understand it.

For all except 2-3 days out of her hormonal cycle/month, she wants someone who is familiar... someone who will provide her with security. And then there's the 2-3 days in that month where she feels sexier, she wears sexier clothing, she puts on bright red lipstick, and she looks at some men and says, "I could do him," points at another, "I could do him," points at another, "I could definitely do him."

This is a time in her menstrual month referred to as 'estrous'.

Estrous in the animal world is also known as mating season. While interestingly most animals only have sex when they're in estrous, the human female has evolved/adapted to be able to have sex even when she isn't in estrous. Most women can't tell when they're in estrous, and most men certainly can't tell if their woman is in estrous. Women have evolved this way for a very important reason...

Here is an excerpt from an article called, "The Double Life Of Women" from Psychology Today:

Over the past decade, evolutionary biologists and psychologists have uncovered abundant evidence that women do, in fact, provide clues to the timing of ovulation, the moment when an egg is released and ready to be fertilized.

Though these changes are far subtler than those in other species, they have a powerful effect on women's perceptions, preferences, and behavior—and the reaction of others to her.

Monthly shifts even affect men's feelings and actions. Indeed, the invisible but influential turns of the reproductive cycle shape the everyday behavior of us all. "Human ovulation is not an observable event, and men and women have no explicit awareness of it," says Martie Haselton, associate professor of communication studies and psychology at UCLA. "But the effects of the menstrual cycle on human behavior are surprisingly strong."

Take, for example, women's preferences in male partners. We may think that each woman has an unchanging "type"—but it turns out that women prefer quite different kinds of men depending on whether or not they are fertile. In the two days or so of the ovulatory phase—the time when women are most likely to become pregnant—they gravitate toward men with more "masculine" traits. That means a man who sports a leaner, V-shaped body, and a face with a squarer chin, straighter, heavier eyebrows, and thinner lips; one who speaks in a lower pitched voice, and displays more aggressive, dominant behavior.

When a woman is in the follicular or luteal phases—during which the uterus sheds its lining and then builds it up again, and in which she generally cannot become pregnant—she prefers men with softer features, less-defined bodies, higher voices, and a gentler manner.

So pronounced are these preferences that Thornhill and his University of New Mexico colleague Steven Gangestad have proposed that women actually have two sexualities: one when they're ovulating, and another during the rest of the month.

These distinct modes emerge out of two competing reproductive goals. "Women want to get the highest-quality genes for their children," says Thornhill, and high genetic quality in a man is indicated by his degree of testosteronization—the extent to which the male hormone testosterone has affected his brain, his face, and the rest of his body.

Once she is pregnant or in the non-fertile part of her cycle, however, a woman's aims do an abrupt about-face: She wants to secure the most generous and stable source of goods for herself and her offspring. Now the nice guy provider starts to look appealing. "When women are in what we call the extended sexuality phase, their preferences shift towards men who appear to have a willingness to share resources like food and protection with her and her children," says Thornhill.

The influence of the menstrual cycle on women is apparent not only in whom they desire but in how they act. Women who are in the ovulatory phase show more interest in erotic materials than women in the luteal or follicular phases; given a choice of movies to watch, they select ones with more romantic or sexual themes.

They take more care with their appearance, and they choose more revealing clothes to wear. In 2004, a group of researchers from the University of Vienna digitally analyzed pictures of 351 women going out to Austrian nightclubs and collected a saliva sample from each. Women whose clothes were tight or showed a lot of skin had higher levels of estradiol, a female hormone that is elevated around the time of ovulation.

It even appears that ovulating women are more receptive to the advances of men— handsome French men at least. In a study led by psychologist Nicolas Guéguen of the University of South Brittany, 22 percent of women in their fertile phase accepted an attractive man's invitation for a date, while only 8 percent of women who were not ovulating said yes.

Perhaps the fertile women were open to a stranger's overtures because they were feeling especially good about themselves; studies by Martie Haselton and others have found that women judge themselves as sexier and more attractive when they are in the ovulatory phase than at other times of the month. And they may actually be more attractive.

Women's faces and bodies undergo subtle changes over the course of the menstrual cycle, research reveals. On fertile days, their voices go up in pitch, their breasts become more symmetrical, and their waist-hip ratio is accentuated (the ratio of the circumference of a woman's waist to that of her hips is a marker of general health and fertility).

Subjects shown pictures of the same woman taken over the course of a month pick the one from her fertile period as the most attractive, and men offered T-shirts worn by women in different phases say that the one worn during ovulation smells best.

Whether they're responding to biochemical cues like body odor, to changes in women's appearance, or to women's altered attitudes and behaviors, research shows that men act differently according to the menstrual phase of the women they encounter.

A study by Thornhill and Gangestad reported that a man with an ovulating female partner is more likely to engage in mate-guarding behaviors, such as paying close attention to her whereabouts and calling her cell phone at random times to see what she's up to. He is also more agreeable in his interactions with her, and more likely to give her gifts.

One of the most arresting studies of male responses to female fertility cues was conducted by Geoffrey Miller, an associate professor of psychology at the University of New Mexico.

Miller found that 18 "lap dancers"—strip club workers who perform provocative dances for male customers—who were menstruating earned an average of about $184 per five-hour shift, while those who were ovulating earned about $354—almost twice as much money, offered by clients who were told nothing about the dancers' cycles.

Moreover, dancers taking birth control pills earned about $193 per shift—more than menstruating women, but much less than women in estrus—and their tips showed no variation across the month. "Hormonal contraception places the female body in a state of pseudo-pregnancy, and it seems that on some level the male customers recognized the women's biological status and responded to it in economic terms," says Miller.

Other studies have demonstrated that the pill effectively eliminates the biological and psychological changes associated with estrus, with unexplored effects on women's long-term mate choices.

Modern contraception, then, may be disrupting an adaptation forged over many thousands of years of evolution. But the precise nature of that adaptation remains to be figured out. There are three principal theories, the first of which is known as the "signaling hypothesis": With her tight clothes, alluring scent, and seductive waist-hip ratio, a woman in estrus is sending out a signal not unlike the chimp or the cat in heat.

"Obviously, women who didn't attract mates and have sex when they were fertile were not going to leave behind any offspring at all," notes Kim Wallen, a professor of psychology and behavioral neuroendocrinology at Emory University. Yet there's reason to think that matters are more complicated than that.

Rather than a simple exchange of information between the sexes—the woman communicates that she's ready to mate, and the man obliges— something altogether more shrewd and devious seems to be afoot.

According to this hypothesis, men and women are engaged in an eons-old co-evolutionary race, in which one sex makes a move and the other matches it.

By identifying a female's fertile phase, a male can maximize his efforts to impregnate her and to keep other males from doing the same.

Women, meanwhile, are strongly motivated to conceal the timing of ovulation. If a man isn't sure when his partner is fertile, he can't restrict her movements or limit her interactions. Hidden ovulation also allows females to discreetly mate with different partners, since none of the potential fathers can be sure of the paternity of the offspring.

Her efforts at subterfuge, however, are always incomplete. "It's difficult for women to fully conceal all signs of fertility—some of them inevitably leak out," says Martie Haselton. "We call this the 'leaky cues hypothesis.'"

To read more on this article, go to:
http://bit.ly/doublelife-of-women

So, when she's in estrus, her uterus goes into a different position and is in "sperm catching mode".

This is the time when she can most likely be able to conceive. She is attracted, for evolutionary purposes, to another kind of male… someone who is unfamiliar.

You see, we humans thrive as a species when we recombine our DNA with a different sort, as opposed to inbreeding. This is someone who her biology and psychology perceives as someone who would increase her genes ability to persist better.

This is a time when her body literally drugs her with chemicals that she can't help. If she is in an exclusive relationship, this is when her body will cause her to 'cheat'. At least in Anglo-America, there is a 30% rate of babies being born that the baby isn't the father's baby and the father didn't know it.

LOVE LIBERATES.
IT DOES NOT BIND.

So I say to my beloved, I am a steakhouse and all I provide is steak. It's great steak! But, still just steak. I don't provide any other kinds. My door is always open, your seat is reserved.

If you want pasta, Mexican, Filipino, Chinese, sushi, go out there and get it, because I don't have it. This is as long as you're okay and understand that if you come home early, there might be someone sitting on your table.

This creates perpetual happiness and profound love in my relationship with my beloved because not only do we never take each other for granted, but we also never operate out of obligation.

You see, I don't 'own' my girlfriend and I let her do whatever she wants and whatever makes her happy. Because happiness is something we create for ourselves, I cannot make her happy. I can certainly do things that can encourage, influence, or motivate her to feel happy, but ultimately it will never 'come' from me.

Obligation is horrible and most people don't recognize what it is. Obligation is doing something not because you want to, but because you have to. The counterpart to obligation is commitment; to do something on an ongoing basis because of your choosing and wanting the end result.

Monogamy, the idea of being with only one person forever, makes it so each other are obligated to be with each other. They aren't with each other because they 'want' to be. I don't ever want that to happen.

My beloved is only with me because she chooses to be. I don't own her, she can do whatever makes her happy and I encourage it.

The only reason my beloved will ever be with me is because she chooses to be and she wants to be. I wouldn't have it any other way, and interestingly it's the most incredible feeling in the world, to know that she's only with you because she wants and likes to!

Marriage, as they say, is like a 'union'. And like any union, it exists to prevent from competition. It prevents both parties from being each other's best option. So, when you're in a monogamous relationship, it makes it so it's inevitable that you'll both take each other for granted. No longer will you be her best option, she'll just be with you because she has no choice.

RULE #2

The second rule is that she must do her absolute best to at least get along with my other girlfriends.

This prevents from any infighting, saying bad things about each other, jealousy, starting rumors or whatever.

Essentially, my female friends know about my other female friends, and my relationships are based on OPEN COMMUNICATION.

Open relationships doesn't necessarily mean "open legs" or "open zipper". Open relationships means open communication, based on honesty and acceptance rather than toleration.

It's based on non-judgmental unconditional love for the other person.

I have an amazing, wonderful, beautiful, adorable, intelligent, my beloved, my best friend and primary lover, Brianna, who is my girlfriend, who assume the title of girlfriend. It's the difference between roles and titles.

The ones who have the 'role' of girlfriend are my friends, whom are women, whom from time to time I have playful sexual fun with (that's the best thing about being friends!). The one who has the 'title' of Girlfriend is my girlfriend whom I introduce as my girlfriend to everyone and she does also with me as her boyfriend. My other female friends, I introduce as "a girlfriend of mine" or "a friend of mine."

CONCLUSION

To wrap this up, women who do as they please for their own reasons are judged, decried, and condemned to "have no self-respect and give it away for nothing."

It's absolutely ridiculous, insane, and based on illogical ideas that are based on unfounded misconceptions. Perhaps after reading this, you might consider to open up your relationships and base it on unconditional love – wanting for each other's self-perpetuated happiness.

Spread the word. This book will never come into mainstream publication because of how radical-seeming these ideas are and the many institutions that will stop at nothing so that these ideas are not propagated to the public.

This will require that you become effective in your communication. This book is short for a reason. This entire idea is actually quite simple and since it is based on inescapable reason, you won't be able to remember how you once thought that women who do what they want for their own reasons, as a bad thing.

What may happen now, and most often does, is that these ideas and concepts I've provided you may fight with your preconceptions as your ego fights to keep you where you are to prevent you from embarrassment (also preventing you from moving forward – essentially fear of change), but you'll find that as time goes by, you'll slowly come into comfort with this information and what'll remain is your wondering how you can begin to apply this immediately into your life where you truly CAN have (no matter who you are) happy, harmonious, sexual, and loving relationships.

Read this book over several times and practice explaining it to everyone you know. Share this book. Become good at explaining these concepts and become confident that you will offer people two things:

1. You offer them an opportunity to emancipate themselves, especially women whom already understand this but hasn't found a frame to put around it and a way to explain it.

They will think of you and thank you tremendously as you free them from feeling shame, guilt, and hatred of themselves over things that have no basis on reality whatsoever.

2. You offer people the most important choice: you offer them Hobson's Choice.

Hobson, who used to rent horses in the 1500's, was the first to come up with the "first in, first out" idea that the horse that was first in queue was the one people could rent. He only gave people that option as he'd say, "Take it, or leave it."

Giving people Hobson's Choice is a great thing you can offer people as it ensures a happy, harmonious relationship as they know exactly what they can expect of you.

They either take you as you are, or they don't. Simple. It is a transparent, simple, sincere, genuine, and worry-free way to communicate as the only thing you'll need to worry about is the truth.

If the thing that holds you back is yourself and your ability to become confident and comfortable enough to lead your life along with others to a life you'd love and enjoy as you master your self, your communication, and the skill-sets necessary to get what you want, I encourage you to apply for a coaching session with me at ronebulaong.com.

If you're a woman, recognize that doing what you want for your own reasons aren't something you should ever feel shame or guilt about.

Recognize that the notion and feeling of security is a logical and emotional construct. Finding it anywhere outside of your own control leaves you at an ever-continuing self-doubt and insecurity.

The truth is, our own sensation of security comes from our own control. We alone determine what we can do to get it and how much we feel we have of it. Find security within your own personal growth.

Recognize that the notion of security that you've been taught to crave is something you can create for yourself and the freedom you desire is yours once you forego the need for other people's validation especially when they're not anyone whom you'd admire.

Respect your opinion of yourself more than anyone else's. Hold yourself in high regard. While there are many people out there that will judge you, recognize that seeking the approval of others whom you do not admire is literally insane. Your happiness comes from you and you alone.

You can be happy right now for no reason than to choose to be happy. Create your own successes. And find and cherish those that will love you unconditionally who will not judge you and who will want for your happiness, joy, self-love and self-actualization.

APPENDIX I: SEEKING APPROVAL FROM OTHERS

It's an awful, sad, unfortunate thing most people do not base their decisions on reason and self-confidence.

Rather, they base their decisions on fear of what other people might think of them, that they may or may not get approval from people they don't even know (nor admire), or by the rules they're surrounded with that they didn't think through, are obsolete, or doesn't apply to them, of the thing that they decide they would do.

It's a crazy thing to seek the approval of people you don't know, you'll never get to meet, or at least that you don't even admire. Seeking the approval of anyone whom you don't admire is quite literally, insanity.

The 'game' of life is pretty simple, but because we live in a consumer world where you're told you're not good enough the way you are, and a societal culture which condemns anyone who doesn't follow it's pre-set rules, that it escapes most people...

If you feel good about doing something and it makes sense to you, logically and emotionally, it's reasonable... then do it. Any notion of guilt or shame should have no place to reside because you have reasoned confidence.

Having this confidence, you'll be able to go up to anyone and reason with them - and the smart individuals will recognize you're right.

You can actually become happy and pleased with yourself all the time once you've controlled what you can expect from others, what others can expect of you, and what you expect others can expect of you.

Once that is absolutely clear and communicated, all that's left is that you decide to be happy (because it's something you decide to do - as opposed as something you get from other people or things), and that you continue on the road towards your own goals.

While others continually strive to become something that they aren't for the sake of pleasing other people, one should continually change (because remaining the same isn't useful at all), but also continuing and becoming more and more oneself to the point that people cannot find holes in your reasoning and confidence because you know exactly who you are, other people know exactly what they can expect of you, and you've communicated it so well, they can't find any holes in your self-confidence.

APPENDIX II: COMPLETE FREE WILL & CHOICE

If someone doesn't 'want' to be with you, why would you make them or force them to be with you in any way?

Most everyone rely on illogical and insane rules based on the premise that: "So that I can have the security that they'll be mine and "love me forever", there must be rules, promises, or contracts, to *bind* them to me... therefore protecting me from any competition, protect me from having to do my best to be their best option, and making sure they don't leave."

(Inevitably leading to the death knell to any loving relationship: that each other take the other for granted)

I take an entirely different stance. A woman will only ever be with me out of complete free will, her choice, with eyes open, open communication, and because she wants and likes to.

The central theme of that kind of worthwhile, unconditional love relationship is that I am worthy, I continue to be worthy of her love, friendship and affection, and I persist to always be her best option with the many option open to her.

Along with that premise is also her understanding that I'm only with her because she's my best option amongst my many options.

In fact, I want so much for her freedom and self-actualization that I will never allow her abdication of her freedom to choose! And usually the women whom are open and prepared for this kind of independence are those that are emancipated, self-validated, self-happy, and self-successful (as opposed to one whom is insecure, validation seeking, life sucking, inexperienced, immature, and narcissistic).

APPENDIX III: WHY THE 2 RULES?

Q: "I'm just curious to why you wouldn't be any woman's only lover...if she chooses you .... I believe men do the picking but women do the choosing...."

A: Great question! I'll answer that in two parts.

Relationships go through the three "i's". Infatuation, Intensity, & Intimacy. Mutually exclusive relationships begin with these three I's where there's a high amount of infatuation, high amount of intensity, and low amount of intimacy (intimacy being your knowing everything about that person).

Infatuation is the chemically bolstered state your body becomes filled with in the beginning of a relationship where you don't see the person for who they actually are. Your mind blocks you from doing so.

This is the stage when you see everything in the person as "cute" or "adorable" or "hot". They can essentially do no wrong.

The reason why 50% of all first marriages end in divorce and 70% of all second marriages end in divorce is because they get married right at that infatuation stage (that lasts up to 18 months) where they make a decision to create a life-long contract of exclusivity while their body is drugged, chemically altered ("under the influence" of infatuation, so to speak). If you were to make any decision while you were under the influence of drugs, the courts would throw it away!

Intensity in the relationship is high in the beginning. You have sex twice a day and maybe 3-5 days a week. Eventually, as the levels of intimacy climbs, the levels of intensity declines. Soon, you no longer have sex as much. Soon, life becomes more important. Soon it becomes once a week. And later it becomes once a month if that. For the majority of people, it becomes a few times a year.

Intimacy is when you really know that person for who they are, mistakes and all. If you're able to accept them exactly as who they are, then it'll work... but even then a lot of things come into play.

One is that the human is sexually attracted to and more successful as "mutts". Meaning, we do better by being a diverse species and survive better through replicating with what we can "recombine" with that enhances our ability to survive genetically.

This is why women have adapted to have two particular portions of her "month" - her menstrual month. Around 28 days out of the month, she looks for someone who provides security. Someone who's "familiar". 3-5 days out of the month, she is in estrous - what's called in mammals as mating season.

Females are the only mammals that can have sex anytime she wants and also one who doesn't advertise her estrous (as opposed to other mammals who advertise when she's ready for sex).

During her estrous, her uterus goes into "sperm-catching mode" and changes positions. She gets very horny and she's attracted a different sort of male. She's attracted to someone who's unfamiliar.

If she was in a "socially exclusive contract", her body will overwhelmingly drug her and might cause her to break that contract secretly.

That's why women grow up having to become good at equivocation... because of the ridiculous societal rules put upon them that they have no choice but to follow (hence the "double bind").

So people come up with ways to 'create' intensity in their relationships through adventurous experimentation. That's essentially what BDSM is for (Bondage & Discipline, Dominance & Submission, Sadism and Masochism). To increase intensity. Some people swing. Some people lie or fight to create intensity and then have "makeup sex" after. All this to create intensity.

The second part...

The reason I wouldn't - correct that; COULDN'T - be any woman's only lover is because, ONE of the reasons is that I only believe in the true kind of love - that is unconditional love.

Quite simply and elegantly, wanting for her happiness intrinsic to my own happiness. No notion of jealousy. No notion of ownership. None of the bogosity society has made up rules about over thousands of years for men to own woman.

And on the other hand, our intensity is always high. She doesn't take me for granted and I don't ever take her for granted.

Because now, she has choice (as opposed to *having no choice* in a monogamous relationship)... and if she's with me, it's only because she CHOOSES to be with me. Nothing else and especially not obligation.

Obligation creates resentment. Doing things not because you want to, rather because you have to.

Commitment is the opposite. Commitment is doing things you have to because you want to the end result.

APPENDIX IV: EMANCIPATED WOMEN

Q: "Do you ever find that it's so hard to find women like that in such a superficial city? Let alone have a real conversation with women in a more intellectual level...

Also, I get the whole "man has to court woman" concept. But I find myself disagreeing with the fact that women aren't as clear with their intentions. It's almost as if you have to captivate and catch their interest first before you find out if they like you back or not. Really though, women need their other half just as much. To me it's almost arrogance.

I understand that you have to show that you are interesting to the other gender because that is part of what will keep you wanting to know more about the other. But I find the man doing this more so than the woman. This should be 2 way, don't you think?"

A: Hey man these are very good questions. Well it's actually not hard to find women who understand my ideals... in fact, almost anyone 'gets it' as soon as I talk about it.

Whenever I talk about these radically different re-approaches on love, sex, and relationships - because it's based on irrefutable and 'inescapable' reason.... most of the women I talk to get it right away.

Simply because they're women and they've never had an actual reason as to why they feel the way they do about certain things (women, having all their life, know that if they make their own decisions and act on it in our society, are taught to feel guilt, shame, and decried by their peers especially other women) until I've helped walk them through some of the fundamental aspects of love, sex, and relationships that they haven't been able to recognize before (enlightenment; to literally to shed light upon something).

I've found a way to communicate it in a way in which also I get to filter whom I decide I want to participate in my lifestyle.

There's no doubt, communicating this takes some communication skills like the stuff I teach in my coaching. It'll take your knowing what you're talking about and having the ability to transfer the data over to her. It's actually very easy once you've learned these and women will love you for emancipating them.

I have girlfriends who'd tell me, "I wish more men were like you." And seems to be the theme of why I do what I do.

The courting dynamic is a very reasonable one - only if you truly understand how it works. Most everyone do not understand this: the woman (rather, the feminine energy) seeks to be led by the man.

The reason why 'worthiness' is the central theme of my existence is because whichever way you see yourself in your own eyes, the feminine energy will follow it. If you think you're not good enough, the woman will think you're not good enough.

While I do teach my girlfriends how to communicate openly with their intentions with a man (only because most men are just horrific with dealing with beautiful, emancipated women), it isn't actually something the man has to need to want from a woman.

The man simply must learn how to lead the woman into adventures she'd enjoy. It's exactly the thing that woman desperately crave in a man, among a few other things.

It's also really important to note that I love and only choose to have relationships with women whom have high self-esteem, are self-happy, and self-actualized. These tend to be women whom are self-successful, emancipated, are beautiful, sexy, sexual, and have a lot of choice in men, whom have foregone the need for other people's approval for them to feel valid and actualized in themselves.

Women whom have low self-esteem tend to compensate for their low self-estimations with judgmental, cynical, and approval seeking behaviors that which I want no part in my life and lifestyle... so the process that I filter out people in my life is very simple and it works out quite well!

While it would be nice to work to emancipate everyone, it isn't worth my time and that focus takes away from the people in my life whom I love tremendously that deserve my attention.

It's good enough for me that these kinds of people hopefully come upon my writing and hopefully open up an insight in their mind that begins a radical change of self-belief and outlook in life.

Your final question has *projection*. Projection is creating an idea you have about yourself and 'casting' them onto others.

Men project.

They think that because their attracted to a woman for her looks, therefore it makes sense to him that he needs to look good. You see, I don't worry about my looks at all. In fact, I never ever try to be impressive.

The only actual reason I work out at the gym is to have actual muscular functionality and structural integrity with my body - as opposed to what most men do in the gym, which is to look good.

60 seconds into a conversation with a woman, she forgets about what I look like because of the things I talk about and the way I present myself. When someone's trying to be impressive, they're not actually being impressive.

Trying is the opposite of being.

Instead, I'm worthy, interesting, and believe intrinsically that their becoming a part of my life and mine becoming a part of theirs will provide so much value, love (the unconditional kind), and growth that I couldn't possibly imagine them thinking their life would be better off without my being a part of it.

It's important for men to recognize that what attracts men to women and vice versa are different and that he mustn't project onto women and think that they're attracted with the same things. In order for men to 'get it up' is for the woman to be (1). attractive enough, and (2). willing.

So he projects that women should be attracted to the same things, that if 'he's' attractive enough and willing, women should be attracted to him! But, in fact, women aren't attracted in the same way. Women need to be 'aroused'. I'll leave it at that

APPENDIX V: ONE NIGHT STANDS

Q: "I got a couple questions and I'm curious as to what your opinion is. What do you think of one night stands? And rather, what do you think of one night stands that turn into something more?

This also begs the question of whether or not it's right for a man to treat a woman this way? But that also relates to whether the woman values herself enough to commit such an act (I guess the same would apply for the man).

Is it still wrong if it was obviously in total mutual agreement? Or do you find this "trashy" or tacky?

More often, people regard women who sleep with many men as "slutty", although the same cannot be said for men who sleep with many women. I guess my question boils down to...

Would you have a one night stand? And what are your values/morals/reasoning behind it? More-so, do you agree with relationships that may sprout from one night stands?"

A: Really great questions! I NEVER have one-night stands. I ONLY have 'First-Night Stands'.

You see, if I find I've connected with a woman whom I've found attractive, compelling, interesting, and valued enough to seek to thrill her in bed, of course I'd love to have a profound, loving, worthwhile, lifetime-long friends relationship that might even grow into something more, following the "2 Rules" model of relationships.

It's important I communicate to her SHE IS SOMEONE I PRICE VERY MUCH and would love to have as a friend and lover (of course the best part of being friends is having sex) and maybe even consider to become something more significant later on.

She realizes that I recognize and appreciate that she's someone who's emancipated enough to act on the things SHE decides she likes, seems to be the arbiter of her own life regardless of what society would think of her, and someone whom, because I'm ABSOLUTELY TRANSPARENT IN MY COMMUNICATION, I've decided I like AS A PERSON.

Remember, society has, over thousands of years, have taught (trained) women that they were supposed to be owned by men. This is of course ridiculous and insane.

Marriage has always been about the vending of a woman to a man - and it's only very recent in the span of history that it was more about the woman's decision.

Therefore, any woman whom would make HER OWN decisions, is the ultimate arbiter of her own life, and act on her own decisions without seeking the validation of what other people would think of her, as she recognizes these things would go against what society expects of her, as they brand her, demoralize her, and scream at her: "You're giving it away for nothing! You have no self-respect!"

And they call her a nasty, evil, four-letter word: a slut. Which, if it were the situation for a man, it wouldn't make sense to him.

This is how our society teaches woman to feel about themselves - profoundly negatively for doing the things they want for their own reasons.

And I work very hard to emancipate woman from this societal oppression - this idea that "they must find their security from a man".

When I find a woman whom is emancipated, I am so incredibly happy, because I've decided long ago that there were women whom I really liked but had to work really hard to emancipate their mind, wasn't actually worth my time because *there are many other someone's* I could be enjoying and sharing my adventures with!

Doing this requires absolute, transparent, clear communication which is, in my opinion, the basis of a wonderful, loving, worthwhile relationship whether if it were an exclusive or a non-exclusive one.

A 'Relationship' is the interaction between two or more entities.

A 'relationship' between a cat and his master hasn't a need to be clear, but more an implicit one and doesn't really require a need for an explicit one.

A 'relationship' between an employee and his employer is one where it's very beneficial for both entities to be absolutely clear as to the relationship and the details of the relationship of both.

A relationship between two people (or more) stands in between, but always stands to become better and more harmonious when the relationship is clear. So it's important for me to communicate very well and that my girl-friend understands exactly what she can expect of me and that I never present myself as anything other than who I actually am.

I am radically honest and truthful and am this way ALL THE TIME. So much so that everyone knows exactly what they can expect of me and I am alarmingly, VERY consistent.

ABOUT THE AUTHOR

 Rone is a transformational leader, master teacher, author. His life's work educates, inspires, and empowers men and women to become comfortable and confident enough in themselves to be able to lead a life of happiness and abundance for themselves and their partner (or partners).

He creates and leads transformational courses that guide people to enlightening their relationships and mastering their minds.

Rone's blend of linguistics, neuroscience, psychology, socio-biology, and design human engineering, combined with his in-depth understanding of attraction-wisdom, creates an integral learning environment for his students.

A certified master trainer of neuro-linguistic programming from Richard Bandler, a master of hypnotherapy, and timeline therapy, Rone's company is a global academy offering powerful transformational lifestyle changes helping men and women to become more and more themselves; annihilating their inhibitions, therefore becoming capable of winning the game of life.

To continue your journey on your self-knowledge and enlightenment, visit his social media's (search Rone John) where he has videos, archives, blog posts and elite-level services on particularly the areas of relationships and personal development.